CURE FOR FEELINGS OF FAILURE

EZEQUIEL N. RICHARDS

Cure for feelings of failure
    Richards, Ezequiel N.
    Cure for feelings of failure/ Ezequiel N. Richards, 2024

    humanidadeemtexto@gmail.com
1. Emotional health 2. Motivation 3. Life project 4.Life review 5.
Action.

LEGAL NOTICE

Cure for feelings of failure

"Emotional health should be the most desired asset for all those who go through the dilemmas and difficulties of the 21st century."

Opening

We need to be honest. In today's world, it is very difficult to be free from the feeling of constant failure or the fear of failing. Low wages, underemployment, housing difficulties, divorce, and emotional illnesses are just some of the features of our generation. In addition to the increasingly expensive cost of maintaining a basic standard of living, we are forced to compete in practically every area of our lives. There is always the feeling that we owe something, and we hear the famous phrases that begin with "you have to": "you have to get married," "you have to have children," "you have to get a better job," "you have to do a postgraduate degree," "you have to travel," and "you have to buy a house.".

It is humanly impossible to achieve all the goals set by society. To be a good father and mother, to be a good partner, to be a great professional, to have enough money to do everything you need and provide pleasure and luxuries. We must remember that we are in a reality where many citizens struggle daily to earn the basics for living and get a decent home for their family. I don't want to talk here only about one-off failures, such as losing a job, failing a test, going through a divorce, or getting into debt. We know from many other books that these situations can be important opportunities for learning and getting back on track. I want to go deeper and contemplate those who have constant failures, who contemplate their own lives as a succession of disappointments to the point of declaring, even in the silence of their rooms, "I'm a failure!" People who are very far from their own dreams and far from the potential they recognize in themselves, who are disappointed day after day and may have lost hope of seeing better days.

I wrote this book for you who can't stand feeling like a failure or a fraud any longer. You may feel this way, even though you have fought honestly until now doing everything right. On the other hand, you may have a little guilt for your current situation for making bad decisions and having screwed up and ruined everything. Unfortunately, that's part of it. Life is made up of mistakes and successes. It is necessary to move forward.

I desire to bring comfort and peace of mind to everyone who reads these pages, as well as to offer a solid foundation for a new perspective of life, where it will be possible to redesign the path, recalibrate expectations, and be happy.

I will not offer any magic solution for success here; I don't believe in it. I have also felt like a failure and experience difficulties on a daily basis. Despite having had great opportunities, having studied at the best schools, and having completed master's degrees, I am far from my field of expertise with no prospect of returning, where I worked for more than 15 years. I used to be very good at what I did, and I believe I still am, but I am currently following new paths. I also wonder if I am successful in my personal life as a husband, father, and friend. I used to think, "What do I exist for?".

Despite all this, I still wake up in the morning and look forward to the day. I still have hope; I am still living and not just surviving. When something goes wrong, I make new plans and goals. I rejoice with those around me; I don't turn down opportunities; I constantly move and reinvent myself. I try to be the best at what I do, even if it's just small household chores. I reflect a lot on what gives me this strength and what motivates me, even though I live in a context that is very different from what I imagined for myself. What is the secret to continuing to love life and reinventing yourself, despite the harsh reality? In the next chapters, I will outline a path towards contentment and a full life, offering tools that will certainly help you see the world differently, with more courage and continuing to seek what you believe life still has to offer you. I will list seven essential steps that will free you from the feeling of failure and help you see a promising future. It will be possible to understand and comprehend the mechanisms of society. Do not accept living dejected, sad, without strength, and without hope. I invite you to follow me on the next pages; you will not regret it.

SUMMARY

FIRST STEP: *Calibrate your perspective*

    Our environment

    Our expectations

    Values.

    The power of gratitude.

SECOND STEP: *find your own individuality*

    Educational system.

    Divergent minds.

    Individual characteristics.

THIRD STEP: *evaluate your story so far*

    Humility.

    Clear mistakes.

    Unintentional mistakes.

    I am grateful for the past.

Forth step: *escape from distractions*

    Competitiveness.

    Media and consumption.

    Social networks.

    Focusing on what matters

Fifth step: *value what persists*

    People.

    Knowledge.

FIRST STEP:

Calibrate your perspective

You certainly know that the idea of "success" and "failure" is relative. It depends on our worldview, our goals, our society, and our history, among other factors. What may be a success for one person may be a failure for another. Even though we are aware of this, when our plans go wrong, we are overcome by a frustrating and overwhelming feeling that blinds us and prevents us from looking at reality objectively. Our emotions work like this: they mix things up so that we can no longer distinguish causes, paths, and solutions. We become incapable of critically analyzing the moment with maturity. Our goal in this step and in the next ones is to bring clarity, putting everything into perspective so that we can see life in a healthy and motivating way.

Our environment

A factor that directly affects our concept of success is the environment in which we live or in which we were raised. I will give some examples to make this clear.

A young man, the son of illiterate parents, may see a university degree from a low-quality college as a great victory, the greatest success of his family. On the other hand, a rich young man from a cultured family will see this same course as a defeat since he was unable to get into a renowned college. He will see many people around him with better educations and will feel resentful.

A young woman who grew up in a very traditional and religious environment will be happy to marry quickly and start a family with three or four children. Meanwhile, another woman who had a different education will look at this young woman with pity, imagining that she will never achieve professional success and will have a frustrating life. On the other hand, the same young woman may look at this successful professional woman and feel the same pity, thinking, "She will never feel as satisfied as I do.".

I remember a time when I worked in a distant and poor neighborhood, leading and helping people. Their standards were so different from mine that I ended up learning valuable lessons. That population was simple and faced many hardships, but they continued to live and celebrate every small victory. Once, a man told me, very enthusiastically, that he was thanking God because he had finally managed to finish plastering his house. In fact, it was a tiny shack on his family's land, where there were already other homes. He was beaming; he had achieved what many in that neighborhood considered success: building his own house and managing to plaster it. He was feeling the taste of success, becoming a dignified person in that place. It was a shock of reality, because at that time I was complaining about the price of rent in the middle-class neighborhood where I lived and was looking for a larger apartment to finance. To understand that group of people, I had to review my values and put myself in their shoes, living that reality. On another occasion, in that same community, we had a problem with a drunk young man who came in shouting and causing a disturbance. He keeps saying:

Do you think I'm worthless? But I'm still going to succeed. I'm going to live in an apartment in that little building, and then you'll say I've succeeded in life.

The mentioned apartment was in a popular complex built by the government for poor people. Was the dream of most of the residents in that area. For him, living there was success. In that environment, I was seen as someone remarkable, even though I didn't consider myself that way. I lived downtown and had a nice car. It was something most of them couldn't even dream of.

Looking into perspective, it seems absurd that someone who has already achieved so much luxury continues to feel like a failure, while another person who lives in poverty feels proud for such small achievements. But we know that's not how it works. What's around us shapes us and defines our values, so much so that it's practically impossible not to feel sad when we don't reach those standards.

Despite having personal dreams and being different from each other, our environment tends to shape us. Even those who decide to confront their local and family culture end up being pressured to fit in if they don't want to spend the rest of their lives seen by others as inadequate.

Years ago, I volunteered as a clown at a large public hospital for about two years. It was one of the best and most rewarding experiences I've ever had. I'm happy to have helped many people smile and find relief in times of difficulty. But the truth is that in that situation I learned more than I helped. I visited them once a week, and every time I left feeling different, grateful for my life. Many times, while putting on makeup, I thought about my problems, but when I finished my shift, they seemed so small that I forgot about them. Unfortunately, I had to stop this activity when I moved to another city for work.

I dealt with people who had been hospitalized for months, confined to their beds. Many lived in other states, which made it difficult for relatives to visit. They certainly had many dreams and expectations for life, but the disease came along and everything changed. The mere visit of a clown performing magic and singing was the highlight of their days. I also saw many parents who were devastated by the hospitalization of their children. All their dreams were left aside because what they wanted most was to see their child alive and healthy again. I remember the orthopedics ward generated the most conversation. In general, the patients were concientes and had undergone surgeries that required a long hospital stay, with the application of pins, prostheses, and other surgical procedures. These people said that their lives had been interrupted by an accident and everything had changed. They had to rethink all their plans, and now their main goal was to get out of there. The ward that used to shake me the most was neurology. When the organization's leaders sent me there, I used to take a deep breath. I knew that I would meet men and women who had undergone skull surgeries, had lost movement, had seizures, were in a state of senility, and were in other similar situations. How could I leave a situation like that without rethinking my concepts and putting my problems into perspective? How could I complain about life and the lack of money when dealing with people whose greatest dream is to stop feeling pain, to walk again, or even to see their child alive?

One thing was common in all hospital visits: practically all the patients I spoke to said that their lives would be different when they left. They had new dreams and created new values, always with expectations of a simpler life, valuing their health and family over great achievements and successes. The environment of pain shaped them and put everything into perspective. I don't want to be like the mothers who resort to news of children going hungry to force their children to eat lunch. Just looking at those who are worse off is not the solution, because there will always be someone in a worse situation than us, that's for sure. I tell these examples, in fact, so that you can reflect on other people's experiences and add these lessons to your own. This can encourage you and make you look at life not only from the perspective of your environment, your bubble, but also broaden your horizons to the point where you can be more independent of the imposed standards. I even invite you to meet different people outside of your own circle. It could be another culture, another social class, another profession, or even another political spectrum. Engage in activities that will help you expand your horizons.

Our expectations

Our environment leads us to form life expectations. In some cases, the parents, since early age, are enchanted by their child's potential and invest in countless activities and courses. They make speeches in front of the child, saying that he or she will be very important and will achieve great things. For someone who grew up hearing this from their family, it is much harder to realize in adulthood that these expectations did not come true, or at least not as imagined. In addition to the real problems, they still carry the burden of having disappointed their parents, family, friends, and society, even if everyone tells them otherwise. Family expectations can be the most diverse and even absurd. I once met a very beautiful young woman, within the aesthetic standards expected by society. Her mother raised her by saying that, with her beauty, she would certainly marry a rich man and have a nice life. This "prophecy" became more and more an obligation. The years went by, and she still did not meet the rich man. She wasn't even dating, while some of her friends were already thinking about getting engaged. This wouldn't have been a problem if it weren't for the expectations created from an early age. This young woman, even with her whole life ahead of her, with great health and beauty, was already starting to feel like a failure.

In other cases, even if the pressure did not come from family, friends, teachers, and the community in general end up creating it. If a child stands out in childhood, he or she gains the reputation of a "child prodigy." Whether in sports, arts, or sciences, every family has one of these children, every school, and even every classroom. The problem is that most of these children will not excel in adult life in the way that was promised to them. So, even if they have a good job and are able to support themselves, in addition to living a peaceful family life, they will feel frustrated for not having achieved power, fame, and wealth. I have seen many family men with stable lives complaining about everything and hating those who, for some reason, "prevented" him from reaching where he thought he could.

It may be that you had high expectations because you managed to go to a good college when you were young or got a job thinking that you would have a meteoric career, but the current results are not what you expected. It is something that happens. Sadly, we see so many people with master's degrees and doctorates, without jobs, without expectations, having to make money from informal work.

I will take the liberty of citing a story from the Bible that may well illustrate the theme we are developing. It does not matter whether you believe in its veracity or not; I simply want to reflect on a narrative that has had a great influence on the Western world and that shapes thinking. The story tells that Moses, despite being the son of slaves in Egypt, was raised by the pharaoh's daughter and grew up as part of royalty. He probably learned all the science of the time and had every opportunity. When he realized the reality of his people and his privilege, he decided to act. He believed that his status would lead him to become a great savior at that moment. He ended up murdering an Egyptian and had to go into exile to avoid being killed by the authorities. Forty years later, we find an elderly Moses in another location, shepherding his father-in-law's flocks. It is at this moment that God decides to call him to free his people. However, he no longer has the expectations he once had. He became someone so overcome by feelings of defeat and inadequacy that they decided to deny the call of divinity, appealing for someone else to be sent. They claim that they are not fit for what is being asked of them and that they cannot even speak properly.

In the culture where the writer sets the story, there is nothing wrong with being married to a wealthy wife and taking care of her flocks. So why does Moses feel so much like a failure that he is certain he cannot do the job? Because of the frustrated expectations of the past. Someone else, in his place, would be happy and readily accept the privilege that was being offered, but not him. He had already let failure take over, living for forty years bitter about having lost everything and not having become what he thought he would be. This feeling almost made him miss the opportunity when it actually arrived. The story above can be a metaphor for a life marked by frustrated expectations and great losses. It makes us reflect on how much the feeling of failure can hinder us and even destroy us. Later on, we will return to Moses again. For now, I want to make you reflect on the expectations created by yourself or by others. Is your sadness today a consequence of projections and fabricated speculations that did not come true?

Values.

Have you ever thought that the environment in which you live certainly contains toxic principles? I'll go further: have you ever considered that your learning may have been impacted in some way by beliefs that end up harming you today? It takes a lot of courage to question what has always seemed so solid to us.

It may be a delicate task to offer a list of worldviews that are harming you, but I invite you to reflect on the values that were learned and that no longer serve you today. They are out of touch with reality or are even doing you harm.

Ideals of power and beauty, for example, are highly valued in our culture. On the other hand, there is an entire movement that questions these standards, and many seek to free themselves from them. I will cite some examples without making value judgments about what you should or should not adopt for yourself: seeking a simpler life; women valuing real bodies; refusing to buy vehicles that pollute the environment; refusing to get married or have children; women who do not shave; men who cry and share their weaknesses; refusing to buy purebred animals.

What we believe about social status can be very harmful. Deep down, many of us still tend to believe that those who do not have possessions are inferior and deserve to be left aside. Those who think this way will be overcome by despair when, due to some circumstance, they have to lower their social status or if they realize that they will not be able to rise as they would like. I have met many poor people who even accepted being treated with contempt by others because they had the exact same values within themselves: only those who have money deserve to be treated with honor. Thus, they continued to be abused, maintaining the dream of one day earning money in some way and deserving dignity.

Standards that define success can be tied to unrealistic and impossible expectations in today's world. When you realize that some of these were part of your education, it is time to review your values. Many have even managed to achieve the goals proposed when they were raised, but when they get there, they still feel frustrated and dissatisfied. What you understand by success can even be something that harms you. I have counseled and supported several couples who had the ideal of success in their marriage. When marital problems began to appear, a feeling of personal failure arose.

I recently counseled a young woman whose biggest dream is to get married. She is professionally successful, healthy, and has many friends, but she feels that she will only be someone when she walks down the aisle as a bride. She has just gotten engaged to a man who is not good for her and who is already showing clear signs of being a possessive abuser. Even so, she insists on getting married and will not accept advice against it, not from me or her family. Getting married is very good; I am living proof of that, but moving forward when things are so bad shows a previous worldview that is harming her today. She needs to rethink what she has learned about what success in life is.

The values imposed by society are very cruel. They hurt and make people sick. The pursuit of the much-dreamed-of success has already caused thousands of people to take their own lives, including teenagers who are taking college entrance exams or who are unhappy with their bodies. If you still carry the idea that people who have not achieved a certain goal are inferior, you will end up hurting not only others but yourself. Keep pursuing your dreams, but do not evaluate the humanity and dignity of a human being by what they have or have not achieved.

The power of gratitude.

Our surroundings certainly normalize lifestyles and impose standards. It would be very naive of me to ask you, the reader, to ignore these values and accept living far below what you are used to. In fact, not even I can do that. Once we experience good things and get used to luxury, it is almost impossible to go back, and when we do so due to external forces, we are overcome by the feeling of failure. For a long time, I had difficulty, for example, understanding families I knew who were reluctant to sell their vehicles when they were in need. They preferred to get into debt or even give up more important things, such as health insurance, rather than having to use public transportation again. I thought that if so many can live without a car, these families could too. However, today, with a child and accustomed to having my own vehicle, I would have a very hard time getting rid of my means of transportation, especially because I need to take my daughter to various places. Even though I know that most don't have the same privileges as me, the possibility of being without a car would still scare me.

Some things can change with age. When we're young, we make sacrifices that, after a certain age, seem impractical. Sleeping in precarious places to save money, eating junk food for meals, traveling with little or no comfort, not going to the doctor or dentist, sharing a room with many people, and sharing a bathroom are some situations that I no longer see myself doing. For refinement or love for my own body.

My proposal in inviting you to look at everything from another perspective is to make you grateful for what life has given you so far, even if you're still fighting for more. There's nothing wrong with seeking improvements and recognition; it's healthy; it shows that we're alive. I'm not advising anyone to be satisfied with the current situation.

Being grateful is very different from being satisfied. I can have lost everything and still be grateful for what I once had and for the conditions that I still have left. Gratitude will not stop me from continuing to seek growth, but it will prevent the feeling of failure. After all, I am in a bad way, but I already have something to hold on to. It could be health, family, a degree, among other things. Gratitude prevents me from seeing only defeat in my life; it makes me focus on what is still good and the tools I still have to move forward.

In recent times, I have ended up losing some things and have regressed a few steps materially. I am struggling to be able to give my family an adequate financial condition again within the context in which I live. I have not given up, and I have not settled. But, at the same time that I look at what I want, I am also happy with what I have already had. It is certainly much more than most people. The fact that I still have the tools to seek makes me very privileged. I have decided that the feeling of failure will not defeat me, and the values of the environment in which I live will not steal my joy. I will continue to be grateful.

SECOND STEP:

Find your own individuality

There are many human beings living on this planet, each one with their own individuality that sets us apart from the rest. It is possible that some of us may look like others physically, so much so that from time to time we see people becoming celebrity doubles. However, our personalities are unique, including our upbringing, our tastes, our way of thinking, our way of building relationships, and our dreams. All of this makes us special; there is only one of us. A great difficulty arises when we come across a system of society that favors standardization. There is a tendency to demand uniformity of mentality, behavior, and tastes. We strive to fit in with what is expected, but we do not always succeed.

The mass culture ends up privileging those who fit into a certain standard or who strive to pretend daily that they can fit in. Those who are unable to follow the majority end up being left aside, missing out on many opportunities.

I am not saying that all your problems arise from non-conformity. In fact, you may define yourself as someone who is well adjusted to what society expects. But it is also possible that you feel like a failure because, to some extent, you have not adapted. In any case, reflect on your personality in relation to the culture in which you are inserted. It will certainly help you to establish more solid foundations of self-understanding and plans for the future.

Educational system.

Historically, the educational system has been geared towards just one type of student: those who concentrate, can sit still for hours in a chair, are disciplined in their studies, and are good at the main subjects. Today, we see new alternatives and other ways of approaching education, but they are still few when compared to the large number of students. The form of education experienced by most of us about two, three, or four decades ago was formal and mass-produced. In systems like this, different people don't have a chance. For example, those who have artistic intelligence end up struggling to fit into the system of classrooms, desks, blackboards, and written tests. The same thing happens to those with practical intelligence, who, as adults, will turn to "hands-on" work. If they don't find someone to stimulate them, particularly along the way, they will experience a series of frustrated attempts and will certainly have this feeling of not fitting in and failure in adult life.

I studied at a school geared towards college entrance exams. Everything involved grades and competition between students. We were even forbidden from doing physical education, as we would be wasting valuable study time. I ended up developing well in this system, which I considered excellent and exemplary. Years later, after evaluating the damage that this system had done to the minds of so many of my classmates, I began to question whether it was really the best way to educate teenagers. It only worked for one type of person. For the rest, it was terrible suffering. I saw many of my classmates go through periods of depression and eating disorders, all due to the pressure of school. Today, when I read news about school and university students who take their own lives, I identify the patterns I experienced during my adolescence.

Many people reach adulthood feeling inadequate, considering themselves incapable of completing the same tasks that others. This is due to the failure of the educational system, which does not consider the differences between us all. Today we know of many recognized geniuses from different fields who had a school life that took their particularities into account and, as a result, almost gave up. How many other geniuses ended up giving up!

Think about your school life. What were the difficulties you faced? It may be that your feeling of failure began way back and that you have not been able to shake it off. If this is your reality, the problem was not you but the system. The first piece of advice I give from this is: do not blame yourself or feel inferior for something that is not your fault. Your particularity should have been taken into account; your unique way of understanding the world should have been considered by the educational system.

From now on, by better understanding some of the social mechanisms that harmed you, you can restructure yourself and seek ways of growing and learning that are more suitable for you. This is the second piece of advice I give. We live in a new reality with countless alternatives. Pedagogy has advanced in such a way that, in many courses, there is now space for teaching methods that take individualities into account. Likewise, advances in technology make it possible to study individually, with the possibility of taking private classes remotely or using distance learning platforms, where you can study at your own pace, in your own way, using the resources that make you most comfortable. Take advantage of this new reality and continue seeking growth, but this time in a way that makes sense to you.

Divergent minds.

The health field, including medical science and psychology, has produced several advances in terms of understanding human beings. Behaviors that were previously seen as "laziness," "tantrums," and "selfishness" are now considered intrinsic special conditions—different types of brain functioning. Here I cite countless situations, such as traumas that influence behavior, neurological diseases, psychiatric cases of all kinds, and even people on the autism spectrum.

I have spoken to mothers who have had their children diagnosed with ADHD (attention deficit hyperactivity disorder) who said, "If they had known this back then, my life would have been very different." If today it is still very difficult to understand how people with ADHD work, imagine what happened in the past. Something that can be controlled with therapy and medication was once a cause of personal failure. Another situation we often see is people with learning difficulties, such as dyslexia, who need therapeutic support in several areas. Many were labeled as incompetent and lazy and gave in to dropping out of school. I have heard health professionals say that there are cases of homeless people who ended up in this situation because society did not understand their condition. These are cases of minds that function differently in a mass-produced system.

I once met a very intelligent teenager, brilliant in fact, but who could not study and did not even have the energy to think about going to college. Unable to understand herself and without the understanding of her family, she was accepting to live an average life, giving up any achievements, and resigned to being supported by her parents. Some friends, finding this situation strange, began to investigate her behavior and convinced her to go to therapy. It was then discovered that she had very intense depression, which had started in puberty and had been with her ever since. With therapeutic and psychiatric care, this young woman began to have more willpower and began to make plans for herself. She had an invisible illness, a medical condition that until then had been preventing her from developing. Unfortunately, this condition is much more common than we imagine. If you have identified with this condition, seek help. There is treatment.

Currently, there are a large number of psychiatric illnesses that affect part of the population and prevent a full life, in addition to depression, among them, we can mention: bipolar disorder, borderline personality disorder, panic syndrome, anxiety disorder, obsessive-compulsive disorder, and schizophrenia. Many who present characteristics of these illnesses have not yet been diagnosed and suffer daily trying to find "normality" on their own, but without success. Science already trains health professionals to deal with issues like these, containing damage, minimizing symptoms, and producing well-being. I am not a doctor, so I do not dare to explain each one in detail, but if you have a behavior that is harming you and preventing you from living, seek help immediately.

There is the situation already mentioned here that is not an illness but another form of behavioral functioning, the autism spectrum. In the past, only children who presented a classic picture were diagnosed with autism: motor difficulties, speech difficulties, abrupt behaviors, repetitive thinking, and other more obvious characteristics. However, as studies have progressed, it has become clear that many autistic people do not present obvious or easily identifiable signs. Observing daily actions ends up offering clues about neurodivergent behavior. I am being very simplistic in my definition, as this is not the focus of this book. But I want to warn you: many autistic people are living without a diagnosis and suffering without understanding why they cannot fit into patterns. Some possible characteristics are: difficulty in making or maintaining friends; being seen as selfish; reacting differently to stimuli; repetitive behaviors; rigidity in plans and routines. If you are in doubt, seek out a serious psychologist who is qualified to apply what they call a "neuropsychological assessment." It is extremely important to understand when our inadequacy and our failures are not our faults. I once heard from a psychiatrist that receiving a diagnosis of autism in adulthood can save a person from suicide.

Whether or not you have a diagnosis or any apparent problem, your mind works in a unique way and may or may not be adapted to what society establishes as typical behaviors. It is important to know yourself so that you can only demand what your body can offer and not blame yourself for situations that are beyond your control. But what should you do after understanding how it works? Start looking for activities and opportunities that best fit your condition. Everyone can be a good professional, as long as they find the right field. Everyone can have good relationships, as long as they understand themselves and the people around them understand their actions. I strongly advise against continuing to try to succeed in situations that harm you and even violate your personal characteristics. Know that your mind is unique, but there are people with similar characteristics. Who knows, you might find a good business providing services to people with the same mental functioning and interests?

If you do not face the conditions described here, pay close attention to the next topic.

Individual characteristics.

I have wondered if I have any issues or even if I am autistic. I have not sought a test, especially because I do not fit into many descriptions. But I have a very peculiar characteristic that has hindered me a lot in my professional life: difficulty in interpersonal relationships with strangers. I find it easy to give lectures and speak to large audiences. I also have personal friends, and I am happy with my family. But, when I meet a stranger in the elevator and need to have some kind of conversation, I panic. I have been in situations of great social contact where I had to greet everyone, and I felt sick and dizzy and had to retreat to a secluded room. This has always caused me great suffering because we are relational and society expects this of us. I know of many professional opportunities that I have lost because I could not maintain the same level of sociability as others. Imagine my difficulty in a job interview, for example.

It took me a while to realize that this is a characteristic of mine; that is how my mind works. I continue to try to improve and behave as expected in different contexts, but I no longer consider myself a failure for not being able to get to where others have gotten to using conversations, jokes, and other relational mechanisms. I cannot be someone else, nor do what my mind is not prepared to do. For a short time, I can even disguise myself, but keeping up the pretense for a long time is an exacerbated suffering that I am no longer willing to go through.

Once, I was moving to another city because I had accepted a new job. I was excited, dreaming of success and thinking that all the problems I had would be left behind. I told a lady I met during this transition about my excitement, and she told me, with all her wisdom, "Be careful, because usually when we move, the problems follow us, because we are the problem." At the time, I thought about it, but I ended up forgetting the advice. Much later, working in the new city and facing very similar problems, I remembered those words. In fact, the inadequacies are mine, and, wherever I go, I will take them. Now I'm dedicating myself to work that respects who I am, which makes me much happier.

This is my characteristic, the part of me that doesn't fit into society. In other aspects, I manage well. Find out what it is about you that doesn't fit in and start putting less pressure on yourself. Keep trying to improve, but don't reach the point of suffering. If things aren't working out even with a lot of effort, it's time to ask yourself if there's something in you that's sabotaging you—a characteristic that's preventing you from enjoying the same things as others. If this is the case, stop beating upon yourself. Get to know your individuality better and start looking for what suits you best.

THIRD STEP:

Evaluate your story so far

Looking back is an important step to free ourselves from the feeling of failure. It is not about dwelling on the past but rather learning from everything we have been through, whether mistakes, successes, justices, and injustices. Are you able to describe everything that has gone wrong so far that has led you to the current situation? Can you point out what your actions were in these situations? The main question of all is: from now on, what will you do differently and what will you continue to do the same way?

Someone might ask if it is possible to be cured of the feeling of failure by remembering everything you have done wrong. Firstly, if we are sincere in acknowledging our mistakes, we will be able to differentiate them from what happened to us and was not our fault, and we will be less demanding of ourselves. Secondly, when we are able to isolate the mistakes and understand the mechanisms that led us to them, we are able to chart a new course, avoiding falling into the same situations. Analyzing the past will give you tools to organize your future and feel confident about it.

Humility.

There are many possibilities to analyze our past. The optimistic ones, which emphasize only the good aspects, and the negative ones, which do the opposite. There are also those that try to be realistic, with more accurate descriptions of situations, but which can be either self-blaming, assuming the blame for everything, or victimization, placing all the blame on others and the system.

It is necessary to have a lot of humility to see our past in an honest way. Recognizing our real mistakes and our share of the blame requires courage. Without it, we will continue to deceive ourselves and make the same mistakes. It is true that we are victims most of the time, but it is also true that we have flaws, and sometimes very big ones. We are human beings; it is impossible for us to go through this life without making mistakes. On the other hand, if you think that everything is your fault, take it easy on yourself. There is a lot of evil and injustice in the world, and we are certainly affected by all of it.

This step aims to evaluate our failures. It is extremely important that you consider everything with humility, ready to recognize your weaknesses.

Clear mistakes.

You want you to remember your obvious mistakes, those that are easy to point out, at least looking from the outside. Many are going through a turbulent professional situation because they did not prepare themselves as they should have, even though they had opportunities. They stopped studying, did not care about the necessary training, and prioritized momentary pleasures. Now, they are feeling the pressure of all the time wasted. Others did not behave in the best way. They lack patience, are arrogant with their peers, have used physical violence, and, as a result, have not been able to secure a job. There are also those who are impulsive, who throw themselves into projects without the necessary preparation, not doing the math. They end up reaping failures and have seen businesses go bankrupt. Today, there are those who have lost everything in betting and gambling, as well as those who fall into chemical addictions. In the family area, some people today feel lonely because they pushed away the people who loved them in their youth, and now it is too late. They were unfaithful to their spouse or violent; they did not show love to their children and saw them drift away; they prioritized business over family. All of these situations, and many others like them, are real failures of people who are now reaping the consequences of their actions.

If you don't identify yourself with this and you're not to blame for what happened to you, move on to the next topic. However, if you've realized that a good portion of your current situation is due to your bad choices, don't despair. Recognizing your own mistakes is already a big step towards transforming your life. When I understand exactly what I did wrong, I'm able to change course and try to get things right from now on. Yes, there's still life and a lot can happen; this will be the topic of the sixth step. For now, focus on what you want to change. A good strategy to make sure you understand what needs to be done is to write it down. Make a list of your mistakes and, next to it, outline strategies so that none of them happen again from now on.

Writing is a mark, a personal document that will be kept as proof to yourself of your commitment. When the same desires return, your written plans can help you block them. It's not possible to cure failure or the feeling of it by constantly making the same mistakes.

In fact, changing is not as simple as it may seem, and you know that. You have certainly tried to do things differently when you realized that you were destroying your life, but you ended up falling into the same situations. When this happens, we are dealing with addictions—choices that we make even though we are sure that they will destroy us. Addiction can be chemical, but it can also be related to other compulsions, such as sexual, gambling, the desire for power, violence, emotional dependence, etc. These end up becoming escape valves when we are faced with suffering. It is difficult for someone to get rid of an addiction alone. In addition to the support of friends and family, therapeutic monitoring and frequent support groups are necessary in many cases. Humility is essential in this process; we recognize that we are sick and need help. There must be a support group near you, whether in a medical center, an NGO, or even a church. Research, seek out, and go without fear.

There is still a valuable warning. Change does not happen overnight. It is a process that varies from person to person. Relapses can happen, which will not mean a return to failure but rather a step back on a long journey forward. Therefore, your focus cannot be on others or on the perfection you want to achieve, but on how much you have already improved. If you fall, get up and continue to walk. Be careful with pride; it can be the main enemy for those who are seeking change. When we succeed and see progress, the tendency is to consider ourselves invincible, and that is when we fall again.

I followed the life of a man who had lost everything due to addictions and violence. He was divorced, had no contact with his daughter, and was unemployed. He had moved back in with his parents and even lost his friends. When he hit rock bottom, he decided to change, and in fact he did. He became a new person, friendly and loving. He met a girl and got married. He went to college again, got a large number of clients, reconnected with his daughter, and managed to rent a nice house. Everything in his life was going well, and that was when his humility ran out. Little by little, he started to distance himself from his new friends, stopped responding to messages, and threw himself into work. I ended up going two years without any further contact and learned from third parties that he was in the process of getting a new divorce because he had cheated on his wife. He also had the same issues again as before. Unfortunately, our ghosts continue to haunt us. We need a lot of willpower and a lot of humility to overcome our daily battles.

If change seems like an impossible mountain to climb, think about the challenges of now. When you wake up, remember that your goal is to try not to make mistakes or hurt anyone that day. To be the best you can be. The next day, wake up with the same purpose. One day at a time, our life is moving towards success.

Unintentional mistakes.

Analyzing the past with courage and humility also makes us realize our unintentional mistakes, the errors we made while trying to get things right. Some of them cannot be considered mistakes in all situations; they depend on the context.

A loving mother is essential for the healthy growth of a child. On the other hand, an overly loving mother can be a problem, suffocating and overprotecting the one she loves. Parents often make mistakes while trying to get things right. If they come clean and are honest, they will realize they overdid it. This is what we should do when we analyze all our actions.

Many relationships fail due to possessive behavior or jealousy. A boss can be reported for demanding too much of his employees or being an extreme perfectionist. On the other hand, an exemplary employee, if not careful, ends up being labeled a "sycophant" by his boss and sees his reputation ruined. A coworker who is concerned about others can end up being labeled the office gossip. When we embark on a new project, if we don't prepare, we end up failing, but if we prepare too much and wait for the perfect moment, we miss opportunities. That's life; we make mistakes trying to get it right, and that's part of it. However, if the same situation has happened more than once and has harmed us, we are facing a behavioral tendency that needs to be reviewed.

Sometimes, our personal characteristics can get in our way, as we saw in the previous step. Examining our past will help us see when something good in us came to the surface at the wrong time, causing discomfort and trouble. For example, being too sincere can be rude, but failing to say what is necessary ends up being an omission. Being introverted in social contexts can get in our way, as can being extroverted in formal contexts. No matter how good your taste in clothing is, if you don't recognize the appropriate social contexts, you can have problems. Speaking too loudly can be good or bad, as can being too expressive or too little. The list of possibilities is endless.

I have a characteristic that is morally very welcome, but it has always hindered me in academic and professional contexts. I can't accept injustice. When I see something wrong happening, I feel obliged to act, even if the one being wronged is not me. I have difficulty remaining in an environment or being part of an institution that hurts people. In theory, this is nice, but in practice it ends up causing me a lot of suffering because all places have some degree of injustice. Since college, I remember finding myself involved in intrigues that were not my responsibility but that I thought I could do something about. People, knowing about my characteristic, ended up looking for me to vent about their problems and see what I could do. I ended up getting into unnecessary fights and "burning myself" with several influential people. I lost opportunities, and I know that to this day there are people who, when they think of my name, remember my combative spirit. My professional life would have been different if I hadn't been involved in so much controversy. This is a large part of the blame I have for my current situation.

Maturity has shown me that it is still very important to have a sense of justice, but not all fights are mine. Furthermore, in many situations I acted without listening to the other side and, therefore, without having a complete understanding of the truth. I learned that I need to be fair, but without necessarily giving in to the impulse for justice that has harmed me so much. This is an example of an unintentional error. I have evaluated my past and seek wisdom to understand which situations I can get involved in.

I am sure that you also have something like this to share—a striking characteristic that has hurt you. Be honest and evaluate your attitudes in the workplace, at home, in relationships, and in your studies. Remember that for something to be good, no matter how good it is, it will always depend on the dosage and the moment.

I am grateful for the past.

Reliving traumas and looking back can be traumatic, particularly when we are attempting to pinpoint our errors. The good news is that you are still alive despite your numerous errors. It's time to reconcile with your history. If you have hurt someone, you can always ask for their forgiveness and, if needed, try your best to make things right. Without this initiative, I don't see any real improvement. Asking for forgiveness is already a step towards a better future; it is an act of humility that is so essential to your change.

Your acts weren't strong enough to kill you. New opportunities can arise, as we will see in step six. Be grateful for what you still have and for the dreams that are being born in your heart.

Forth step:

Escape from distractions

Something I have learned from leading and advising people is that the human spirit is rarely satisfied. Just as there will always be someone in a worse situation than us, there will also be someone in a better situation. If our goal of success is to reach the top in such a way as to leave everyone behind, we will have a serious problem of constant dissatisfaction.

Imagine that you are in a race with a set route. You have trained, planned, and know what you need to do to reach the finish line in good shape. Suddenly, in the middle of the race, you find out that the prize money for the first-placed runners has changed. Your strategy is then remade. Before it was just to finish the race, now it has become to finish first. A short time later, you discover that the finish line has been changed; it is closer. So you start to accelerate as much as possible. After a few minutes, you are informed that the finish line has been moved again, but to a much further location, kilometers away. Your plans are again adapted, and now, already exhausted, you need to save energy. Would you run a race like this, where everything could change at any moment? It seems crazy. A wise runner would not let himself be carried away by the changes and would only do what he had already planned, to the place that had been previously defined. That would be his personal victory, regardless of how much the others ran or how much they won as a prize.

Why do we accept living our lives as if we were playing this sport without criteria? We dream and plan according to the tools we have and our goals. Along the way, more tempting proposals appear that make us forget our initial goal, and we change the goal. With each new distraction that presents itself to us, we change the goal again and, in fact, we never get there. We may even have reached the initial target, but since the focus has changed, the feeling will not be of victory but of failure.

A person who managed to leave the community where he lived and move to an upscale neighborhood will soon be aspiring to have the same things as his neighbors. When he achieves everything, that neighborhood will no longer be as good because he will be coveting a more luxurious place. The greater the growth, the greater the contact with wealth, and the greater the greed. The popular car gives way to a luxury one, which gives way to a helicopter, which gives way to a private jet, which gives way to a transatlantic yacht. Being a millionaire is not enough; he wants to be a billionaire; then, a trillionaire.

I am not against getting rich; I even admire people who have built great fortunes through honest work. However, I recognize that some of these people still feel like failures because they got distracted and gave up on their initial goals.

Unfortunately, personal life also has these same traps. A person who was previously in a good marriage may start to get frustrated when they realize that someone else's spouse does things that seem better or is even better looking than their own. They may also envy the life of apparent freedom that some single friends enjoy or the constant cases of marital infidelity committed by acquaintances. The old dream of being married with children may give way to the desire to enjoy all of life's pleasures, to travel without obstacles, to return to a youth that was thought to be lost. It is sad to realize how many marriages have ended because one or both parties got carried away by distractions that appear along the way. Later on, when they realize that none of it was solid, it is already too late. Some, out of fear or weakness, do not end the relationship but visibly live frustrated, wanting more than they have achieved because they are looking around and forgetting what really mattered from the beginning.

People can change, and plans can change. We are constantly changing, but we need to be careful that our change is not motivated by momentary desires, excitement, empty promises, vanity, hatred, or envy. Those who move in this way do not achieve satisfaction; they always seek emptiness and will invariably end up with a feeling of failure and regret.

Competitiveness.

Our capitalist culture leads us to compete with each other from an early age. In fact, this already happens in the family itself when parents make comparisons between siblings. Who is the best child, who gets the best grades, who is better at sports, who is more talented, and so on. At school, it is no different. Even in a school concerned with not imposing rivalry between children, comparisons between grades and behaviors are inevitable. In sports, it happens even more. Competition is present, and we cannot escape it, whether in college entrance exams, job searches, professional advancement, or even romantic relationships.

It takes a lot of wisdom to know how to compete in these situations without bringing this spirit into the spheres of personal life. Seeing everyone around us as an adversary is very damaging. Any healthy relationship where one side is competitive will end up being contaminated by resentment when the other party stands out more, gets promoted, or earns more. Friendships end because of envy, families break up, and couples get divorced. You've probably heard a story of a marriage where everything was going well until someone, usually the woman, started earning more money, then problems began.

Why is it difficult for so many people to have a personal relationship with someone who has achieved more? Deep down, they still see everyone as an adversary. I was once talking to an acquaintance and listening to him complain about his life. In his version, everything was going badly; there was no hope. He was sad and shaken. However, I knew him. He had a wife, two children, a house, and some possessions, and they were all healthy. I tried to go deeper to understand the reason for so much distress. At one point, in the middle of an example, he said, "Even my brother, who never studied, has a better house than mine and a better car than mine." I realized at that moment that all that feeling of failure came not from his personal reality but from his projection onto the life of his brother, whom he judged incapable but seemed to have a higher social status at that moment. An unnecessary distraction that was stealing his joy in life and preventing him from fully enjoying life with his family.

I recently heard about a man who hates his profession. When I asked why he was in it, the answer was that his mother was always praising his brother for going to college. To please her and show that he could also bring her joy, he decided to take the same course. And what was the result? He is not happy; he suffers every day doing what he doesn't like, and his mother still seems to like his brother more. Competitiveness made him look in the wrong place when choosing a profession. He forgot his calling, his desire, and his plans. He wanted to be better than his brother in front of his parents.

Bringing competition into our personal lives even takes away the pleasure of rejoicing in the success of the people we love. When we receive news of marriage, pregnancy, job promotion, diploma, trip abroad, and other advantages, we feel resentful, as if someone were stealing a chance from us. We forget that we are different and that life will never be the same for each of us. We have different tastes, aptitudes, dreams, and plans. We also make personal choices that lead us down different paths.

I have also been tempted by this resentment many times. I received good news about someone and wonder when something like that would happen to me. In doing so, I had forgotten all the times that, yes, I had already been blessed with many victories. Now, I've decided to stay focused on my goals and reflect on how my conscious decisions did not lead me to the same paths of someone who was blessed with something, and that is okay.

Perceiving life as a race full of opponents makes us live looking back, to the side, and forward, when, in fact, we should be looking at the target we want to reach. When we look back at those we consider inferior, we are overcome by pride, which makes many relationships impossible. Looking back can also set us back. It can make us stop pursuing what we really want since we are already better than many. When we look to the side, at those who apparently are in the same position as us, we always try to speed up and measure ourselves shoulder to shoulder. When we look at those ahead of us, envy and greed take over, making us run after goals that weren't even ours. At this point, the feeling of failure builds in our hearts when we realize that we can't achieve them.

What do you really want from life? What are you truly seeking? Reflect on this, considering how you can do good for yourself and the people you love. Evaluate your skills, your tastes, and your vocation, and set goals that make sense to you. Run your own race with your own target, without deviating because of the performance of others.

Media and consumption.

For a long time, anyone in society has had to know how to deal with the offering of products that they often don't need. The creation of a consumer market is linked to the advertising of manufactured items that are now intended to be purchased by the public. But for that to happen, they must first be desired. Both commercials and very skilled salespeople present us with something new and try to convince us that it is necessary. Surely all adults today had a childhood filled with toy commercials on the television programs they watched. The wealthier parents, who were able to buy all those trinkets, satisfied the need created in their children. Children who could not afford them, on the other hand, were sad and frustrated, envying their rich friend or relative who had access to them. However, this frustration should not even exist since no one really needed those toys. Television, with its very well-crafted commercials, created that fetish that makes many adults today still feel an existential void and buy everything they see as soon as they get some money. I've heard the phrase a lot: "Nowadays I buy because when I was a child my parents didn't have money and I was left wanting more."

All of this is a great demonstration of what constitutes a distraction that gives us a feeling of failure without necessarily being true. It's no wonder that the discussion about advertising for children is very serious these days. However, we adults continue to be susceptible to this media manipulation. Advertising is still very strong in all types of media, both printed and audiovisual. The Internet has brought it even closer, to the palm of our hands in an increasingly creative way. Luxury housing, clothing and accessory brands, and technological launches are just examples of what has attracted people's attention, more than essential items such as food, health, and education.

Whoever creates the product, markets it, and advertises it is doing their job. It is part of advertising to prove that an object is the best product in the world and that whoever doesn't buy it is a failure. It is up to us on the other side to judge what really makes sense in our lives and what is superfluous. And it gets worse. It is common to link items to an entire lifestyle that is often unrealistic. People who lack financial maturity end up getting into debt and, when they can't pay their bills, feel like failures. Those who have financial maturity but not emotional maturity will redirect their lives by making meticulous plans on how to acquire something that won't make any difference. We find maturity in consumption when we realize that human value is not linked to products. I will not be a better or worse person if I buy or don't buy something. And if you are in a social circle that will stop valuing you if you don't own a product, it is time to review your friendships and the places you go.

Our current situation is so delicate that it is difficult to discern what is truly essential. It seems that everything is important, and we cannot let go. This is not a home economics book, and I do not have the necessary tools to help you in this regard. The best advice I can give you at this moment is: make your plans based on your tastes and values, and do not let yourself be attracted by new releases and launches that take you away from your initial goals. Do not be guided by advertising. Do not let the media tell you what should be important to you.

Social networks.

One of the biggest distractions nowadays is social networking. A quick search on the internet is enough to confirm the number of reports and scientific articles produced in recent years that demonstrate how following profiles on different networks can be a problem and even affect mental health. What was initially just a way of connecting people to each other has ended up becoming showcases of well-being, luxury, success, and power.

On social networks, we post joy, victories, and successes. The photos are always beautiful and filtered, exposing what we want to show and hiding our real lives and the difficulties of everyday life. In just ten minutes looking at the profiles of acquaintances, we get the impression that everyone is well and happy, with great marriages and beautiful children, in good health, exercising, eating well, traveling abroad, and being successful in their professions. Now, imagine how devastating all of this is to be seen by someone who is divorced, unemployed, and sick. In all my years working with the public, I can attest to how much the life shown on social media is deceiving. I've been seeing a lot of beautiful photos of families when, in fact, I knew that there was almost daily abuse and physical violence. How many trips in which beautiful photos were taken actually caused the family debt, putting their children's education at risk? I even ended up noticing a pattern: the more photo posts we see of a couple, the closer they are to divorce.

I learned that the grass of your neighbor is always better because you are seeing it from afar. If you get closer, you will notice the holes, the imperfections, and the flaws. Up close, no family is perfect. If we had any idea of the daily struggle of these people who expose their achievements on social media, we certainly wouldn't be envious. Don't be fooled by this world provided by social media. Everyone goes through problems.

There is also a very important warning about social media. It is increasingly common for us to follow influencers: people who, in general, are not part of our circle of friends but who, out of admiration, enter our lives because we follow their daily lives so much. It is clear that the actions of many of these people are to flaunt their lifestyle and wealth. The more profiles like these we follow, the more we get the feeling that we should fight to have the same things; after all, everything seems so "normal." Thus, a woman who is at the height of her family and professional life tends to feel frustrated because she doesn't have those clothes or can't go on that trip that the influencer always takes. A man who until then didn't see a problem with his wife starts to despise her because her post-pregnancy body hasn't returned to what it was before, like an influencer he follows. People with no apparent reason to complain about life start to aspire to an unattainable status.

It is worth remembering that many of these influencers receive money from brands to advertise explicitly and implicitly, making it almost impossible to differentiate a commercial from a demonstration of daily activity. And when the standard conveyed is unattainable, they promote websites and betting platforms so that followers can keep alive the dream of being like them. We know how much this practice has destroyed lives and families.

How much emotional distress could be avoided if we were wise in the use of social media? In itself, it can be very beneficial and continue to connect people, as long as it does not become an instrument that generates dissatisfaction for us. If you cannot make healthy use of it, perhaps it is better to disconnect for a while or stop following those profiles that are hurting you so much. It makes no sense to access something that is intended to be fun and end up worse off than we already were. Do your emotional health a favor and remove these distractions from your life.

Focusing on what matters

Distraction, by definition, reveals a lack of focus or attention. It can also be a consequence of a lack of motivation or even tiredness. If you have been very distracted in your life, chasing after any new thing that is offered to you, reflect on the possible causes. It may be that you are very curious and fickle about new things and thus end up getting easily fooled. On the other hand, there is the possibility that you are already tired of the direction your life has taken or no longer believe in your former plans. If this is the case, as I said before, there is no problem in changing. Have courage, look inside yourself, at the circumstances, and evaluate what is different. Do not remain in a tiring and hopeless situation. Take some time to get to know yourself better before starting new projects. Without this, you will continue to be distracted, following what does not matter, wasting your time and your money, as well as harming those around you. Once you know your new tastes and where you want to go, rethink your plans with maturity and follow them, avoiding distractions.

One last important piece of advice for those who still have trouble defining their priorities. Look at what has happened in your life that has made you feel good or happy. What kind of work has given you satisfaction, what kind of relationship has made sense, and what good things do you have that make you proud? The way you reacted to what has happened to you in the past can give you important information about your personal taste and what you need to continue seeking in your life. My daughter, like any other child, always asks for lots of things as gifts. However, over time, I have come to realize that some types of gifts attract her more attention than others. Even though she always asks for a pretty doll when she sees one in a shop window, she ends up not playing with it when she receives one as a gift. On the other hand, when she receives books or comics, she reads each one incessantly to the point of memorizing the lines. It is clear to me that the demand for a pretty doll is more related to advertising and the persuasion generated than to a real taste for that object. The book, on the other hand, reflects a real personal taste. What has really done you good, and what have you neglected until now? Start by outlining your priorities and be grateful for everything you have achieved so far.

Fifth step:

Value what persists

Certainly, those who achieve fame end up influencing more people than those who are anonymous, both for good and for bad. However, your existence will always leave its mark, no matter how insignificant you consider yourself to be. When we are in a state of disillusionment, feeling like failures, we forget all the important things we have done. Even considering that we have achieved no success, we have certainly influenced people, acquired knowledge and transmitted it, lived experiences, and made contributions.

The feeling of failure carries with it the idea that our life up until now was worthless and useless. Since I failed to reach my goals, I am led to believe that nothing I have done is worthy of note. This mistaken idea can lead many to a complete lack of hope and even to suicide. How can we continue living if we consider ourselves completely useless?

When we feel defeated, we need to remember what remains: all the marks we have done in the world.

People.

We are relational beings. From birth, we interact with relatives and acquaintances, even involuntarily. Our influence on the lives of everyone around us, even when we are still very young, is part of our legacy.

If you were born into a structured family and it was planned, you have certainly heard that your birth made your parents' dream come true, or at least brought a lot of joy to your family. Even if this is not your case, your existence may have contributed to someone's maturity or to having their life completely transformed. The specific cases of those who suffered abandonment can also be an example. If they are alive today, they had to make connections to survive, even more intensely than others. In fact, if this is your case, know that your life is an example. I greatly admire people who did not have the privileges that I had and still grew and developed. Your example has already marked many lives.

We cannot measure the influence of our actions on the lives of others. Try to remember those who were important to you in some situation. How many of these people have you been able to return a message of gratitude to? Certainly not many. I now remember teachers from my adolescence, leaders, friends, and even neighbors with whom I no longer have any contact but who were important and helped me become who I am today. It is possible that some of these are now feeling like a failure, without even knowing how important they were in someone's life. If you have had family and friends and participated in some community, you certainly made a difference. Don't think about the situations in which you ended up causing hurt and harm to someone. In fact, if this happened, don't repeat the mistake again. But know that, even in situations in which we ended up doing harm, we may have indirectly contributed to growth. However, I want you to remember the situations in which you were a positive influence.

Have you brought happiness to your family? Have you given good advice to friends? Have you helped support someone in need? Have you been a good father or mother up until now? Have you been a good spouse? Have you done a good deed for a stranger? Are you cordial to those you approach? Have you been a good listener when someone needed it? Have you been a good coworker? I could ask countless similar questions, but you can already see where I'm going with this. If you answered yes to just one, it's proof that your life is not useless. Your good deed may have happened in the past, but the marks remain. You touched someone in this world.

Some human interactions have the power to contribute to good even when we don't see it. Not every relationship that ends actually goes wrong. A relationship that has come to an end may have actually worked out well if both parties grew during the time they were together, even if they never see each other again. A teacher who fails a student may have brought much more help than the approval at that moment. A scolding from a boss may have the power to redirect a career, and so on.

Dealing with failure in a mature way is enough to inspire those around us. Everyone understands the joy someone feels when things are going well. However, maintaining serenity and courage in moments of weakness and defeat is something few can do. It is possible that your resilience is impacting people around you. If you stand and keep fighting despite defeats, others will be inspired by your example.

Some time ago, a very dear person was diagnosed with one of the worst diseases in existence: amyotrophic lateral sclerosis (ALS). For those who don't know, it is a degenerative disease in which the patient gradually loses all movement in their body but remains conscious and has all sensations. I saw that lady's life deteriorating. With each encounter, less she moves. At a certain point, she could no longer leave the house, and then she could no longer get out of bed. There came a moment where she was no longer able to move any muscles; she could only blink. Many acquaintances visited her and sang to her. They knew that she liked to listen to songs, because as long as she could speak, she always asked for them. When she was already paralyzed, she would cry when she heard the melodies, showing that she was still fighting. It was impressive to witness her resilience; everyone left there shocked. Some time later, she passed away, leaving a mark on everyone who was with her in those moments. That woman's blinking encourages me to this day, even after she's dead.

You don't have to be famous or successful to make a difference in people's lives. In fact, anyone who follows the lives of celebrities knows that it's common for a celebrity to impact thousands of people but not be able to do good for their own family, being careless in raising their children and forgetting about their own marriage. I decided that the greatest purpose of my life is to take care of my wife and daughter. To some, this may seem like little, but they are my world. I don't want any fame or status that can keep me away from this mission. Make it your priority to impact those who are important to you. After that, who knows, maybe you'll be ready to influence the world.

Knowledge.

Every experience has the power to teach us a little more. Life is a constant learning process. We may lose many things along the way, but the knowledge acquired both through studies and in practical life will remain with us.

Unfortunately, we have developed a utilitarian relationship with studies. We say that it is necessary to have an education to "have a good job." Yes, it is true that a good education can increase the chances of professional success. However, acquired knowledge is not just a marketing tool. If that is the case, everything that was built in our education will have been pointless if we do not get the job of our dreams. In fact, this utilitarian relationship has led many to disillusionment when they realize that, no matter how hard they have tried, they continue to be relegated to a situation of underemployment.

It is very unfair that highly qualified and educated people are in need, while some young people, just by dancing in front of a camera, earn rivers of money. But this is the current reality; our society values entertainment more than education. It would be very wise if we encouraged our children to study not for the promise of financial gain but to become better human beings and for the pleasure of learning more. Some would disregard the advice, but others would follow the path of study, and even if they were unable to turn their degree certificate into money, they would not feel like failures as they do today.

If you have a couple of degree certificates and are still experiencing serious financial problems, keep up the fight. You are not alone in this situation. Do not regret having studied. The knowledge you acquired made you grow, and no one can take that away from you. Your studies may have made you a better citizen, a better son, a better coworker, or even a better spouse. If there is an opportunity to continue studying, go for it. Do not pursue knowledge thinking only in results.

Experiences.

Your experiences so far leave marks that stay with you. They are real situations that remain in your memory and in the memory of those who lived alongside you. Today, these memories are not just abstract concepts; they still have an impact and shape your behavior. The romantic moment, that fantastic trip, the conversation with friends, the news of approval, the compliments received, and so many other experiences we have lived are with us to this day.

It is true that we have both good memories and also desperate and traumatic situations. These tend to scare us and have the power to take away our hope in a different future. I want to demonstrate here a very common inconsistency among pessimists. Bad memories, such as disappointments, betrayals, dismissals, and violence, are pointed out as causes that make us lose hope. However, the same person also feels like a failure when he looks back and realizes that he had great moments but will not be able to repeat them. You have lost the purchasing power to travel internationally; you can no longer be a member of a certain club; you have lost dear friends, among many other examples. Thus, a pattern can be seen. Complaining about life, no matter what happened in the past, whether good or bad. In short, if you have had bad experiences, you complain. If you have had good experiences but you cannot redo them, you also complain.

This highlights a very harmful personal tendency: always looking back with complaints and pessimism. I am not delegitimizing your suffering. If there are severe traumas in your life, I suggest that you do not just read books but also seek therapy. If you have tried to look at things in a positive way but are unable to, I also recommend that you seek a professional in the field of psychology or even in the medical field. There is nothing wrong with that; a truly healthy person is one who recognizes that they have difficulties and seeks help. I am here, in fact, provoking you, leading you to see the privilege of having good experiences and good memories.

Feeling nostalgic for what happened means that we had good times. How many will never experience the pleasure we feel in different circumstances! Good memories have the power to show you that life was worth it.

What is good remains

In this topic, I tried to prove that your past still counts. It serves to show you that your life has value. Even if you do nothing else from now on, your experience on this planet left its mark and made you grow. It is time to be grateful for the opportunity to have touched lives, matured, and lived good experiences. If we are unable to value all the good that remains, we will not have the courage to seek what may still come in the future, a subject we will discuss next.

You are not useless. Even if today you cannot see yourself making a difference, what you have already done will remain.

SIXTH STEP:

Believe Without Giving up

In a world that celebrates achievements at an increasingly early age, it can be very discouraging to reach a certain point in life and realize that we have not yet achieved the success we imagined in our minds.

The daily news usually brings stories about child actors, singers who are already successful in their teens, fifteen-year-old athletes traveling the world and winning Olympic medals, and young people in their early twenties getting doctorates. Parents seeking success for their children enroll them in countless courses, and we see children who are, at the same time, multilingual, athletes, and musicians. We do not know how all this movement will end or what the mental and emotional impact will be on the lives of these children. But when we realize that people less than half our age have apparently already achieved more than us, the feeling is inevitably one of failure. In these cases, time can be a villain. As we age, opportunities become scarcer in a society that values youth and technological knowledge over experience.

In this environment, it seems difficult to encourage someone in middle age to continue fighting for their dreams, especially if they have already experienced countless failures. Even those who have been successful consider that they have lived their peak and nothing better can come from now on. The long-awaited retirement arrives with disappointment and a feeling of defeat.

But what should we do if we have already reached this point and still have health and many years ahead of us? Spending the next few decades resentful and complaining should be out of the question. We need to understand that life is not over. While we are here, many positive things can still happen.

If there is life, there is a chance.

Being alive is a gift. If our health still allows us to do the necessary activities, we have an even greater privilege. Even when it is lacking, life can surprise us. I would like to once again quote a biblical text that motivates me in moments of weakness. It was written a long time ago by a wise man who, after observing life so much, came to a conclusion: everything is ephemeral, so it is necessary to value what we have today. Read it very carefully:

But anyone who is alive in the world of the living has some hope; a live dog is better off than a dead lion. Yes, the living know they are going to die, but the dead know nothing. They have no further reward; they are completely forgotten. Their loves, their hates, their passions, all died with them. They will never again take part in anything that happens in this world.

Go ahead - eat your food and be happy; drink your wine and be cheerful. It's all right with God. Always look happy and cheerful. Enjoy life with the one you love, as long as you live the useless life that God has given you in this world. Enjoy every useless day of it, because that is all you will get for all your trouble.

Ecclesiastes 9, 4-9 (GNT American Bible Society)

No matter how bad your life is, you are not dead. As the text says, it is better to be a living dog than a dead lion. The breath of life brings perspective, hope, strength, and courage. An emotionally healthy human being fights for his or her preservation at all costs. Even living in degrading situations, even torture, people tend to resist and make plans for the future. Because of this, the desire for death can reveal itself in an illness. If this is your case, I suggest you see a doctor to check on your health. Treatment can certainly help you. Don't give up.

While there is life, dreams can be fulfilled, plans can be renewed, surprises can happen, and good news can come. That long-awaited phone call can be received, an unexpected visit can knock on the door, the payment that has been withheld for so long can be released, and even a cure for that annoying illness can happen. The world is full of possibilities.

My pessimistic side made me imagine that the worst would befall me. I used to think that if bad things happen to others, why wouldn't they happen to me? However, lately, I've been led to think the opposite: if good things happen to others, why wouldn't they happen to me too? In fact, both thoughts are correct, but I got tired of only looking at the negative side. I realized that I wouldn't survive if I didn't change my thinking. Now, I continue working and giving my best, waiting with great hope for the moment when I will receive some good news. Is it possible that it will never come? Unfortunately, yes. But while there is life, there is hope.

The wise man's text also advises us to be happy with what we have today. And what a precious word! We spend so much time envying other people's possessions and complaining about our misfortunes that we don't realize the wonders of being alive. The embrace of family, good food, the smile of children, the breeze on a hot day, the warmth of the sun on cold days, refreshing water that quenches our thirst, and the smell of coffee when we wake up are some privileges that only those who are alive can enjoy. Expect good news, but also enjoy the good things today!

The examples are powerful.

Contrary to what we might think, achievements can come at the most varied moments in our lives. It's okay if you're not a young prodigy; there's still time for great deeds.

Let's go back to the biblical story of Moses. That man who failed in his attempt to become a leader of his people was now an elderly man of 80 years old. He was shepherding his father-in-law's flock when he was called to free the Hebrews. He didn't believe he would be capable, nor did he want this task. He was overcome by feelings of failure and complacency. He was probably already counting how many boring years he still had to live. But everything changed. God entrusted his plan to that elderly man, and, in the following forty years, he accomplished great deeds. He is still considered the most important person in Judaism and a very important leader within Christianity.

I keep wondering why a story like this is in the Bible, and then I remember other characters who also stood out after they were elderly, such as Abraham and Sarah, who realized their dream of having a child after they were 90 years old. Regardless of whether you believe the text or not, realize that the Bible, the main book in the West, is telling us that there is no age limit to be successful and make a difference. No one is too old when it comes to being used by God or achieving their dreams.

It is impressive how many successful celebrities have been recognized well into their old age. I invite you to do a quick search on the internet about the subject. I can cite as an example the writer José Saramago, one of the most important Portuguese-language writers of the 20th century and winner of the Nobel Prize for Literature. He became a writer in his youth, combining books with his work as a journalist. However, his first work that was truly appreciated by the public and critics was released when he was sixty years old. From then on, he received recognition for everything he did.

Actor Morgan Freeman is another name that always appears on these lists. He worked in theater with little success until he was cast in a film that made him famous worldwide at the age of fifty. Actor Harrison Ford was a carpenter and only got his first chance in the cinema at the age of 35. Julia Child, the world's most famous presenter of cooking shows, presented her first episode on television when she was already 51 years old. The renowned cartoonist Stan Lee published his first superhero story at the age of 39 and, from then on, created countless characters that are now portrayed in various media.

These are just a few known cases, as there are countless anonymous people who achieved success in their field of business only at an advanced age. If all of these people had given up after their first failures, they would not have achieved victory. A defeatist attitude would have prevented them from continuing to seek the success they so desperately sought.

In the area of relationships, we can also be surprised by what life has to offer us. Many end up finding true love after middle age or even when they are elderly. Our ability to rebuild our lives can surprise us. I have seen betrayed and divorced people who no longer expected anything good have their situation transformed when they met someone unexpectedly.

I remember that for a while I followed the life of a woman who had always dreamed of having children, but without success. She had already been married and separated and discovered that she was infertile. Time passed, and her dreams became a thing of the past. Until, due to these surprises in life, she ended up meeting a widower with three small children. They fell in love and, some time later, got married. The children, even knowing the story of their biological mother, began to call her mother, and at this time I met them. For me, it was a shock when she told me her story, and I discovered that she was not the biological mother of the three. In her words, "I always wanted to be a mother, and my children were already there without me knowing it." These surprises are wonders that only those who are alive can enjoy.

I cannot guarantee that your persistence will bear good fruit and lead you to the realization of your dreams. I am not even sure about that for myself. But I assure you that, if there is life, there is a chance. Have hope!

Re-signifying dreams.

It takes wisdom to understand how much it is still worth persisting in a purpose and when it is time to change course or adapt a plan. Changing a life purpose does not mean defeat. If, for example, you dream of being a singer but you are neither in tune nor charismatic, you may be facing an insurmountable barrier. One solution would be to try to enter the music business in another way: as a sound technician, manager, talent scout, radio host, phonographic reporter, data analyst, among many other possibilities. It is possible to make adjustments to your plans and continue to seek something in the area that makes you happy. Who knows, the secret to getting the chance you have been waiting for is to change your mindset, redefining goals and steps. However, to do this, you need to be humble and recognize that your choices so far have not been the best. It is also necessary to take a few steps back, which can lead to the feeling of wasting time and going back. However, in some cases, without the necessary changes, the results will not appear.

There are situations that require persistence and willpower, while others require a change in attitude or even goals. There is no formula, and the answer may vary. Ultimately, it is up to us to decide how much longer we will fight in the same way to achieve the same dream and when it is time to make adjustments. Constant frustrations can be part of the journey to success, or they can indicate the need for changes. Regardless of your choice, the most important thing is to keep your heart full of hope and know that, if you are alive, anything can happen.

Redefining dreams also requires learning to take advantage of opportunities. Sometimes we are so focused on our initial plan that we do not see great possibilities that may go unnoticed. I have seen adults who regretted giving up unique opportunities when they were young because they thought, "This is not really what I want." Much of the success achieved today is due to the flexible attitudes of people who took advantage of opportunities they never imagined before with the thought, "Whatever happens, I will try." In fact, we don't know everything that exists in the world, nor all the nuances of professions and relationships. We can always be surprised, and if we don't give new things a chance, we will never know. New professions, new products, and with them, new opportunities are constantly emerging. Be open to analyzing new things with great seriousness and wisdom, so as not to miss out on good opportunities but also to avoid falling into scams and traps. Many surprising things can still come your way. Some people end up being surprised by an old video that goes viral, an unexpected encounter with a celebrity that changes their entire life, a marketing strategy that works, or even a job offer that seemed impossible. Keep working, wait, and be grateful for what you have today. Warm your heart with these examples, because without hope we are nothing.

" But anyone who is alive in the world of the living has some hope [...]"

SEVENTH STEP:

Nurture a healthy spirituality

Here I want to reflect on what transcends what our eyes can see and the objective reality of the world: our spirituality.

Spirituality does not always imply religion.

Despite its roots in the biblical notion of God's "breath," spirituality is not always associated with religion. It characterizes our set of life values and beliefs, both enduring and transient. It involves different religious and also atheistic nuances. In fact, without spirituality, everything we have discussed in this book thus far could no longer make sense. With its evil, failures, frustrations, and disappointments, the world's harshness tries to rob us of the beauty that comes from having hope for a better future. It also impairs how we see ourselves and the others around us. We would be utterly consumed by materialism, narcissism, and pessimism if we didn't have our spirituality.

It is healthy spirituality that leads someone to maintain hope in the face of chaos and to continue believing even if all the results say otherwise. It is what allows someone to wake up and declare, "Today is going to be a good day," even if there is no material evidence for it. It makes us take joy and pleasure in the little things and adopt goals for our love.

Personal convictions and the "spirit of the season"

To be able to define who I am, I need to resort to a framework of convictions that involve my upbringing, the environment in which I live, my history, my moral values, and my self-esteem, in addition to my faith related to the religious paradigm that I follow. The same occurs when I define what I expect from life.

Even those who do not profess any religion or even claim not to believe in anything are also driven by standards and concepts that may not be obvious and objective. Likewise, as I said above, faith is only one of the factors that shape us, and it is common to identify people in a certain religion behaving in a way that is contrary to its precepts. Our spirituality involves many elements.

We need to emphasize that there is also a collective spirituality that tends to shape individuals to the acceptable standard. You, the reader, must have already realized that I am a Christian. I see a Christian society cultivating values that are very different from those that can be found in the gospels. These values of today are even spread by religious leaders themselves. This is because there is what we usually call the "spirit of the season," the set of beliefs and values that shape a society at certain moments in history. The concept explains why people with such different religions and even atheists live in the same way, with the same convictions. As the world becomes more globalized, this "spirit of the times" becomes increasingly more comprehensive. There has always been a social ideal about what constitutes a good life, what is acceptable, what is fair, and what is beautiful. And it changes over time.

The vision of what constitutes a "perfect body," for example, has changed a lot over the last few decades and continues to change. In the past, a couple needed to have at least 5 children to be respected; today, this is unthinkable in most families. There was a time when a well-regarded family man was a manual laborer who could bring food home. Today, a thin, pale man who spends all day working on a computer can be someone admired. Being successful was once synonymous with being an exemplary citizen, honest, and debt-free. Today, the concept depends on the accumulation of assets, the zip code, and the bank account, regardless of the number of lawsuits one faces in court.

We need to recognize that these transitory values claim authority and affect citizens who live under their influence, trying to leave no room for questioning and confrontation. They affect disciples of the most varied beliefs and all social classes; they have no boundaries of race or ethnicity, as well as gender or age. All of this powerfully influences our individual spirituality. I believe that your self-definition and your desires for life need to come from your own personal tastes and experiences and not from external insights that aim to manipulate you and lead you in a certain direction, usually in the interest of whoever is guiding you. These are desires and convictions that come from outside, like a graft from another mind or an organ from an incompatible donor, if that is a better metaphor. Suddenly, you find yourself unhappy because you are not achieving something that, in fact, you neither wanted nor needed. You ended up hearing it from someone or were pressured by the environment, and now you consider that you will only be a valuable human being when you achieve it.

I will give an example of what I am describing to make everything more clear. Currently, media and social networks, as we have seen before, are defining what constitutes the standard of success. Based on this, influencers, professional coaches (nothing against those who do serious work), and even religious leaders incorporate these standards into their speeches and impose them on the public that follows them. By listening to these statements, your personality is being nullified, and your objectives are modified in order to try to achieve that goal that is being sold as the only way to success. If you have difficulty achieving it and you are religious, you will begin to think that the deity has abandoned you. Your personal tastes, your talents, and your love for those around you need to speak louder than external influence; only then will you be able to develop a healthy spirituality. You will no longer be taken over by greed and envy that have taken away so much of people's joy. You will desire what really matters and be happy with true achievements. The definition of who you are cannot be based on the values of the "spirit of the times." Nor should your life purpose be a priority to live up to it.

If you have a faith based on a religion and you truly believe that its principles are the best for your life, try to study it more and follow the teachings of the principal historical figures. This will be important to judge the relevance or not of what current leaders are teaching. It will help you see if they are stuck in the "spirit of the season."

The after.

Much of our spirituality is directed towards the future, towards what comes next. Hope is perhaps the main motivating element, which makes us project results and consequences of our actions, as well as dream about what can be improved. When it is lacking, it seems that nothing makes sense.

There is hope based on concrete facts that actually are expectations for consequences. There is also purely speculative hope, coming from an optimistic ideal or from faith in the transcendent. The first, even though it seems empirical, cannot offer guarantees; after all, we are talking about the future in a world of injustices. Thus, a real effort may or may not be rewarded. A young person who studied all year for a college entrance exam has a better chance of passing than one who did not study, but even so, approval is not guaranteed. The second type of hope is even more uncertain, coming from convictions belonging to another sphere of existence. Even so, people tend to base themselves more on this second type.

In the Bible, there is a brief definition of faith, which, even though it may seem simplistic, can help us.

To have faith is to be sure of the things we hope for, to be certain of the things we cannot see.

Hebrews 11,1 (GNT American Bible Society)

Yes, faith leads to firm convictions so much so that we believe as if we had proven it. Convictions about the future set our lives in motion and motivate us, even if current circumstances are not satisfactory. In a country full of injustice, inequality, violence, and corruption, it is impossible to have a full life without exercising faith and seeking hope in it.

There are religions, such as Christianity, that bring in their belief system the conviction of a perfect future life for those who follow the doctrine. This motivating element has supported millions throughout history. It makes them continue to believe that better days will come, here or in the afterlife. Skeptics claim that this is harmful because people direct their lives towards something that cannot be proven to be true. They would be being deceived. But I want to make a counterpoint here. Those who do not have faith in a beautiful future world but who still live a healthy life with expectations also direct their faith in unprovable ideals, such as the belief that humanity will evolve, that human beings will unite, that there is some political ideology capable of bringing justice and equity, that there is a leader or group of people capable of doing justice for the people, that a certain type of battle is the solution to society's ills, and so on. If it weren't like that, these people would have already given up on life. Why continue fighting if there is no prospect of improvement? Utopias are necessary.

Understand that, whether you are religious or not, it is necessary to dream about the future. It may not come true as we imagine, but who knows? Our dreams and our convictions must remain alive. If you are feeling discouraged, take a few steps back and reevaluate your expectations. What do you hope will happen in your life and in the world from now on? If there have been disappointments, I invite you to create new expectations and live with them in mind.

Expectations for today

Our goals cannot be based solely on the future. It is commonplace to say that the path we take is as important as the destination, and I see great truth in this. If we do not reach the goal, what we have done up until then will not have been useless if we have found meaning in the journey and even enjoyed it.

Proof of this are those who regret retirement. They have always dreamed of the moment when they would have money and time to do whatever they wanted, but when they get there, they end up realizing that the day-to-day work, feeling productive, and interacting with people made more sense than the goal itself.

Our convictions dictate how much we need to submit ourselves to suffering in order to reach the desired goal, but without finding meaning and pleasure in our daily lives, life becomes very heavy. In the religious field, for example, there has been much criticism of theologies that lead believers to dream of paradise but pay little attention to their daily lives, offering no tools to endure current suffering or even overcome it. It takes a lot of resilience to live dreaming about the future without getting any relief in the present. Not everyone has it, and those who are able to endure it end up settling for a miserable life.

Jesus himself declared in the gospels that his desire for his disciples was not a life of hardship and suffering.

I have come in order that you might have life - life in all its fullness.

John 10,10b (GNT American Bible Society)

Come to me, all of you who are tired from carrying heavy loads, and I will give you rest. Take my yoke and put it on you, and learn from me, because I am gentle and humble in spirit; and you will find rest. For the yoke I will give you is easy, and the load I will put on you is light.

Matthew 11,28-30 (GNT American Bible Society)

I think the same goes for all religions and beliefs. It is necessary to seek satisfaction and joy, but it may seem that they will only exist if the goal has already been reached. This is a big mistake. I can indeed be very happy without fulfilling the purpose.

One way to live fully even in the midst of difficulties is to understand the reason why I am subjecting myself to certain situations. A person who studies hard 15 hours a day to pass an exam knows the reason for his struggle and his momentary suffering. At the end of the day, already exhausted, he can be filled with hope when he realizes that he is closer to the goal. A mother with a very difficult work routine can face it with a smile on her face when she remembers that, due to her effort, her children will have a good education. What is your motivation? Why are you trying hard today? Finding the reason for our effort brings relief. Suffering for itself has nothing to say except the feeling of emptiness, disappointment, and uselessness.

Little things

Even with clear goals, your routine may still be making you sick. If this is the case, think about whether it is really worth it. There are ways to achieve your goals that do not put your physical and emotional health at risk. New goals can also be set. Our lives are worth more than promotions, salaries, or status. I worked closely with teenagers for over ten years. I can assure you that, as much as money is necessary, what a child or teenager misses most in their life is the company of their parents and their love. Someone who grew up without resources but was loved is capable of chasing their dreams. Someone who always had everything except their parents' love grows up with such a huge existential void that nothing can fill it. In general, they become fragile, dependent adults, prone to depression and possibly addictions.

We focus on the big picture, on the final goal, and forget about the small joys of everyday life. Spending time with those we love, seeing a smile, and giving someone a hug are actions that can very well fill an exhausting workday. The pleasure of watching a good movie, eating delicious food, and talking to friends should impact our days in such a way that we can say that we are happy, even with many problems. Emotional maturity makes me dream of a better future without forgetting what is good today.

Looking at the world in search of what is beautiful is an exercise in spirituality. It brings relief and comfort in suffering. It makes us nurture the attitude of gratitude, so dear and important for those who are going through difficult trials. Cheers! There are still many good things around you; enjoy them.

CONCLUSION AND CONTINUATION

After reading each of the seven steps carefully, you will now have the tools to reinterpret your situation and better prepare yourself for what is to come. The steps we have presented are related to emotional health, something fundamental to all who live in this society with so many challenges and pressures.

These convictions have been with me for some time, maturing in my heart, giving me the courage to persist even in unfavorable contexts. Everything written here is based on personal reflections, life experiences, and a lot of reading. I chose not to mention or indicate books and authors so that the reading would be easier and more fluid, but know that there is support from psychology, sociology, and theology.

The teachings described here reveal the need to understand the mechanisms that move our society, together with your self-knowledge. The reconciliation of these two fields will give you clarity to continue making plans. Therefore, to go deeper and better distinguish the contradictions between these spheres, I recommend reading sociology books that explain the systems that exist in our society and searching within yourself to better understand. Constant reflection and therapy can help you define what really matters to you.

It is also worth noting that this book is not a substitute for therapeutic or medical intervention. If, even knowing all of this and applying these steps, dissatisfaction persists along with sadness, it is worth investigating.

I certainly did not explain all the relevant subjects, and, in some topics, I was superficial. But I hope that the content of these pages helps you and opens your mind to a new world full of possibilities, as it did for me. Do not forget that life brings many opportunities for invention and reinvention and that it is not over yet. You have value; you are someone who has already touched lives and can still make a difference. Keep dreaming and searching; on the path there is already fulfillment and satisfaction.

Final Message

I would like to thank everyone who has come this far. Thank you for your time and trust. If this book has helped you in any way, please share it with friends and acquaintances who may be experiencing the same problems as you.

If you have any questions, criticisms, or contributions, feel free to write to the email below or access the Instagram profile:

humanidadeemtexto@gmail.com
@humanidadeemtexto

I would be very happy if you could make a public review of this book on the shopping site, so that this material can reach more people.

Have a good journey!

About the author

The author of this book is married and the father of one daughter. He has extensive academic and professional experience in areas such as teaching, authoring materials, counseling, leadership, and training. In his work with the public, he has encountered very different life contexts, which has led him to accumulate a vast knowledge about human beings and their social context. He has recently begun to dedicate himself to something he really enjoys, and everyone says he does very well: writing.

www.ingramcontent.com/pod-product-compliance
Lightning Source LLC
Chambersburg PA
CBHW051828250726